God's Gift

What God Sent

I God had sent the miracle of
It was just on to live and
Breath to the work
Of to die on
The cross
The most greatest
Thing in the world his son

The Prince of Peace

His name to be of life
To be true healer
He was to be son
Of the true father

He to himself to
Be the one to
The king of life
Hey saved life from sin

He is son of our
God his name is
The king of kings
His name Jesus

Amen

How to

Heal

How to heal I don't
Know how but there
Is one the healer
Of life on to heal

One to heal the
Blind the one of
Many things no one
To what no one else

That is the reason

Why the true healer
Was born and belief
There is a son

Death can

Rise

He can rise the
Dead he
Can live
And
Die can
He come back
To life yes he can

His Story

The true story of man that
You won't see until
It is your time
His is written
A book
On the
One
Did many
Miracles the one
That Had save lives
From sin of pain he lives

Sin is Saved

Call out to the true one
Cause he took pain
From the one
To saved
Your
Life the day
He lived and died
And came to life on that day

A Story of the True One

It was known through Adam
And Eve after they
Broke the first
Sin to the
Fruit
That he will
Send for a son to
Save lives from sin

He is Always

In pain and when we
Are said for him
Pray he will be
There just call his name

He never stop love
Give your love back
He will love for always
Heart is there he will be

There he loves always
In his is the true
Heart won't break
It will in you

The Name

Was it yours to
Remember or was
His your name always
Be remember cause

You put your name
In his you forget
His name is in
Yours life won't

Forget

Strong in the Weak

Strongest thing one thing
A man can do

Is to be weak
And pain for us to live

Wrong
Crown

It was the wrongest thing
They made the thorns of
Crown on his head
They took nails
To hands
And
Feet it's
Wrong but saved
Me away from pain but
I love and won't forget that man

Cry on That Day

Is your tears for joy or
Sadness life
Was give by one
He lived for us

And for the pain
I cry on that day
It is my life to
Know we are his

You Believe

If you wondering if he
Is around you believe
He will be there
If you go to
Grace
You believe
He will be there
He is yours he be there

Where is
Help

Is anyone there to help
It is the one to ask of
He is the one
Of full help
He mine
And
Yours
His name is
Jesus he is the one of help

What is My life

What is my life for it is for
The one his life the
One in my life
Life is good
It is my
Life
I live
And breathe
I give my life it is Jesus

Is it light or

Dark

It with the day to be light
And night it was
A night the
King had
Came
 It
In light
He breathed
And walk it was a
Day of pain and night
He had died and it was

Light the came again

That Good God

Is he cause he is
God is the one
He is the only
The one god

God sent his
Messagers to bring
Life of the one
On earth his son

That's good God

On the Mountain

On the mountain of life
He slept and awoke
He went the bush
And the one father

Was for the son
To bring the in
Pain he the true
Sacrifice for life

Die and Live

He had die and live
Yes he had died
And yes he lived
He was the son

He lived and died
On the cross
And yes he did
He was our soul

He did save us
All from the sin
And yes he did
Amen

To Father

He lived for father
Did the most impossible
To the he healed
And life to what

He was the one
Only son of the
Father he is the
Imagine of the ones

That knew there would

Be a son the only
One to his father

The Nail

The nail gave life
The nail gave death

It gave life free
Made to repent

The nail gave me
To reborn again
Now I am saved
From life

I God here

What is life it is
Good and his name
Is God he is with in
All he is the holy

Of us all that
Is the reason
He is the all
Might his name is

God

Is God Good

Why is he good?
He made all life
Made all the animals
He made man and women

That is why God is good

Where is Heaven

Heaven is here on
Earth it is in the
Clouds and the sky
Heaven is a second

Place on earth it is
Place of no sin
It is place were
Life lives again

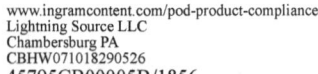